Published by Ice House Books

Concept by Spencer Wilson & Chris McGuire

Illustrations copyright © 2020 Spencer Wilson
Courtesy of Yellow House Art Licensing
www.yellowhouseartlicensing.com

Text copyright © 2020 Chris McGuire

Edited by Samantha Rigby

Ice House Books is an imprint of Half Moon Bay Limited
The Ice House, 124 Walcot Street, Bath, BA1 5BG
www.icehousebooks.co.uk

ISBN 978-1-912867-72-1

Printed in China

Homeworking
THE ULTIMATE GUIDE

PART 1:
MYTH VS
REALITY

PART 2:
HOMEWORKING
HACKS

PART 3:
HOME IS
WHERE THE
HEART IS

HOMEWORKING
(NOT HOMEWORK)

For clarity's sake, this book is about homeworking, not homework.

If you're after a book about homework (poor you), you'll need to search elsewhere. Homework is what happens when Miss Jones decides 10C needs to swot up on trigonometry, or if Mr Baxendale thinks 9G should get to grips with iambic pentameter. The concept of homework was created by sadists with the express intention of ruining evenings and weekends for every child on the planet.

The mere mention of 'homework' sparks fear in adults who, years after leaving school, still lose sleep to vivid nightmares about forgetting to list every form of the French verb 'dormir'. Interestingly, homework was at the core of at least 50% of plot lines in both *Grange Hill* and *Byker Grove*: where it was perennially lost, stolen, forgotten or, horror of horrors, eaten by the dog!

Homeworking, on the other hand, is the process by which adults live a stress-reduced life by doing their job from the comforts of their own home. The two never mix*.

*Except for teachers who mark homework at home – poor souls.

TECHNOLOGY WILL SET YOU FREE

Our brave new world of homeworking is only possible due to the amazing tech at our fingertips. Here's what you need:

The Posh Coffee Machine
The most vital kit in any homeworker's arsenal. The idea of anyone working from home without semi-instant access to a flat white is, quite simply, laughable.

The Video Call
Meet with co-workers and clients without the need to travel. Video calls also reveal the terrible wallpaper in the homeworker's 'office' and the ridiculous things their pets are up to.

The Wi-Fi
Tech that allows the homeworker to be online, without attaching to a cable or port. Some argue Wi-Fi is cooking our brains, but all agree that's a small price to pay in order to send emails from the loo.

The Smart Phone
An office in the homeworker's hand. Write documents, email and more. The smart phone is also handy for selfies, while hard at work of course, to share online with your office-dwelling friends.

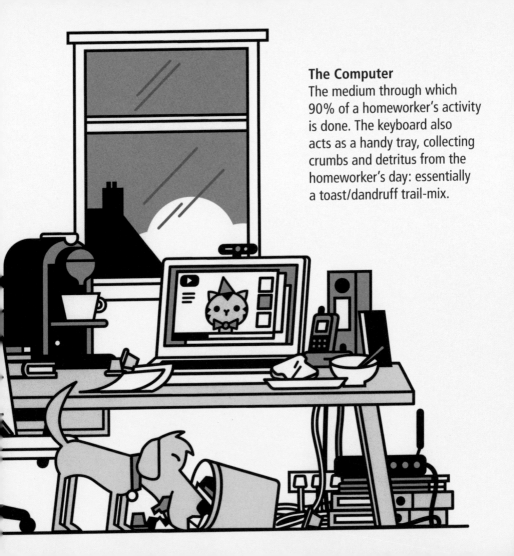

The Computer
The medium through which 90% of a homeworker's activity is done. The keyboard also acts as a handy tray, collecting crumbs and detritus from the homeworker's day: essentially a toast/dandruff trail-mix.

PART 1
MYTH VS REALITY

THE PERMANENT HOLIDAY

The myth states many homeworkers might as well be on the beach, because working at home is just like an extended holiday ... right?

It's an understandable notion, homeworkers (both self-employed and those working remotely) do enjoy not being confined to a specific place of work: they can complete tasks where they want and (often) when they want.

Yet, the incredible truth is, it's still WORK. Homeworkers, despite their location, have the same deadlines as their office-based counterparts. And who in their right mind would take a holiday in a home office? A random selection of mismatched flat-pack office furniture, bulky tech and purloined stationery is hardly akin to the view from a lounger in the Maldives.

THE TRUTH: It's important to remember the 'working' element of homeworking. That said, homeworking can be much more pleasurable than life in a conventional office, and a piña colada or two on a Friday afternoon wouldn't go amiss...

THE HAVEN OF TRANQUILLITY

Without the din of city-centre traffic, the nerve-shattering splutter of the air-conditioning and the drone of Pete from HR (about who's getting custody of the ironing board in his divorce settlement), homeworkers are free to do their job in a haven of tranquillity, right? For most, working in a domestic setting, surely the biggest distraction is the occasional ping of the coffee machine announcing their latte is ready?

The reality can be rather different. Nobody really knows their neighbourhood until they've tried to work there, on a weekday, between 9am and 5pm. Suddenly the nice lady next door magics up seven screaming babies, whose caterwauling is only bettered by Tony at No. 42 – holding a thrash metal festival on his patio. Not to mention Brian, the retired geography teacher, who's trying a spot of fracking in his garden shed.

THE TRUTH: Tranquillity is by no means guaranteed, even in a (seemingly) idyllic suburban environment. The neighbours that the homeworker believed to be Margo and Jerry Leadbetter could quite easily turn into The Munsters. That said, the average homeworker would be desperately unlucky to find themselves living anywhere even half as noisy as the average office.

YOU'LL MISS THE OFFICE

Did you catch the game last night?

After a few weeks, so the myth says, the homeworker misses the energy, cut and thrust of their previous place of work. Soon they'll be pining for watercooler chats about 'the stupid one in *Love Island*' and impromptu trips to the pub (to watch co-workers eat their body weight in pork scratchings). It won't be long until the newly transitioned homeworker discovers watching *Loose Women* with the cat, while gorging on fromage frais, just isn't the same!

The reality is quite different. Yes, some homeworkers miss their former place of work, but only when viewing it through rose-tinted glasses. They soon realise they don't miss waiting hours for a one-page document queued behind a colleague printing off *War and Peace* on the communal printer. Avoiding the necessity to join a huddle around an acquaintance's desk, mumbling through *Happy Birthday To You*, isn't much of a loss, either. Every now and then, homeworkers might take a trip back to the old office and quite enjoy it, but let's be honest, that's because they don't have to go every day.

THE TRUTH: Yes, some homeworkers miss the office – this will pass. There are changes homeworkers must adjust to. However, it's easy for a homeworker to maintain the best relationships from their former place of work, and, with all the extra time on their hands, get to know new people (who they might actually like) in their domestic setting.

HOMEWORKERS ARE TV JUNKIES

Ask the man on the *Blue Peter Omnibus* and he'll tell you: homeworkers spend their days lapping up *This Morning* and *Diagnosis Murder*. As such, they have an encyclopaedic knowledge of the latest, celebrity-endorsed, streak-free self-tanning products, along with a detailed understanding of police forensics procedure.

Yet, the reality is rather different. As the old saying goes: 'Just because you can, doesn't mean you should'. Homeworkers do have access to TV, but it doesn't necessarily follow that they spend entire days watching reruns of *Columbo*. Remember, those who work from home also have constant access to their bath tub, but this doesn't mean they spend every day up to their neck in Radox.

We're not suggesting converts to the homeworking lifestyle never turn the television on during work hours. But gorging on TV quickly loses its shine: there are only so many episodes of *Antiques Road Trip* one person can sanely watch. Homeworkers still have deadlines to meet, tasks to complete and hoops to jump through – few of which are assisted by watching telly.

THE TRUTH: Telly is no more of a distraction than chatting with co-workers or listening to the radio (if you're allowed!) in a conventional office. On the plus side, if there is an unmissable TV event on during the day, from a Royal Wedding to a World Cup Final, there's nothing to stop a homeworker grabbing the popcorn and 'having it on in the background'.

Just one more thing ... you watch a lot of daytime television, don't you.

THE 'NO FIXED HOURS' SCAM

Homeworkers log on when they fancy it, log off when the whim takes them ...

... or so the myth says. It's all about getting away with doing as little as possible. 'No fixed hours' equates to VERY FEW hours, right? As essentially the homeworker's boss is paying them not to show up?

You must have so much free time!

The reality is rather different. Yes, many homeworkers choose their own schedules – but most have 'core hours' when they're expected to be available. Homeworkers still have tasks to fulfil and deadlines to meet just like the regular 9-to-5 crowd.

Remember, sitting in a busy office for 8 hours a day does not necessarily equate to being a superior worker. Anyone who's worked in a traditional workspace knows how easy it can be to while away the hours online or quietly playing *Solitaire* on a small, easily-hidden browser window.

Homeworkers, without the numerous distractions of a traditional workplace, work smarter than their conventional colleagues – getting things done quicker and to a higher standard. They don't spend hours gossiping with the boss's PA about *Ru Paul's Drag Race*, nor do they kill time creating unnecessary tasks (reorganising the stationery cupboard twice a week). In a conventional office, it can sometimes be all about looking busy – for homeworkers the focus is on actually getting work done.

THE TRUTH: There's no doubt some work from home in order to play the system – getting by on doing the bare minimum of work – but these are the minority. Most simply use their lack of fixed hours to fit their job around other commitments. Homeworkers tend to be driven, working smarter, in order to make the most of their time.

THE 30-SECOND COMMUTE

> I bet you roll out of bed at ten to nine.

Nobody enjoys their commute. It's a potent little package of hell served up twice a day, five days a week. But the homeworker, it would seem, has beaten the system, right? They wake up at 8:50am, step into slippers and wander across the hallway to the home office. Moments later they're sipping coffee and playing with the cat, while their computer powers up. At 8:51 the homeworker is ready to go, feeling smug about the countless hoards fighting in traffic to be at their desks in the next 10 minutes ...

Yes, working from home makes life less stressful around rush hour, but the reality is most homeworkers still have hectic mornings. Those with kids still have to get their sprogs up, washed, fed and out to school on time – and get back in time to start working.

Then there are other household tasks to master: cleaning last night's dishes, hanging out washing, working out if that 'funny smell' has anything to do with the dog. When your home is where you have to work, suddenly tidying up seems more urgent.

THE TRUTH: The quick commute may exist for some, but most homeworkers find there's a multitude of tasks to carry out while everyone else is stuck in traffic. That said, they're still likely to be a fabulous improvement on being stuck in a car, bus, train or tube carriage for several hours every day.

PART 2
HOMEWORKING HACKS

SORT THE WI-FI FIRST

Working from home without effective Wi-Fi is like competing in the Tour De France without a bike: it's just a terrible idea – chocolate teapots and inflatable dart boards have nothing on this one!

Before anyone considers relocating their work life they MUST ensure their home tech is fit for purpose. Checking their home broadband speed is vital. Prospective homeworkers should pick the fastest broadband they can get, even if it's the most expensive. The amount of anxiety a bad broadband service causes is so great it's always worth the extra expense to upgrade!

Those planning to become homeworkers need to think about where they're going to be working, too. Setting up office in a goat-herder's shack may sound bucolic, but it'll be a nightmare for homeworking if there's no phone signal or broadband.

Those ignoring this advice shouldn't be surprised when their work days are blighted by files that take an eon to download; phone calls that have more snap, crackle and pop than a breakfast cereal; and video-conferencing harder to follow than the latest Scandi-Noir drama. While they're at it, potential homeworkers should make sure their computer works flawlessly and they've invested in a printer that doesn't take until Christmas to deliver a three-line memo.

Finally, and probably most importantly, there's coffee. Homeworking without access to really good coffee is like jumping out of a plane without a parachute – something that's only ever attempted once.

LOVE THY NEIGHBOUR

Homeworkers quickly become aware who in their locality spends most of their time at home. It's crucial to make friends with, and 'manage', these residents.

Otherwise, Mr Simpson's desire to sandblast antique furniture every morning (creating a sound like a jet taking off) or the woman at No. 24's decision to burn industrial waste every Tuesday, smoking out the neighbourhood, may completely derail any homeworking plans. It's important to make neighbours aware they're not the only ones in the vicinity during the day – the homeworker is there too, trying to get some work done. Hopefully this information, combined with any presents the homeworker gives to sweeten the deal (e.g. bake some muffins), might (fingers crossed) make their neighbours think twice before embarking on any particularly antisocial activity on weekdays.

The important thing to remember is, whatever a homeworker may be tempted to do, they should NEVER EVER fall out with the neighbours. This can be disastrous, ruining both the homeworker's home and work life: it's not like those who work from home can escape to their office in the city for 9 hours every day. If things go sour, homeworkers and neighbours are stuck with each other.

*A final thought: anyone who comes out to their neighbours as a homeworker will, inevitably, find their house nominated as the back-up parcel delivery point for the entire neighbourhood. Take it on the chin – it comes with the territory.

ALWAYS HAVE A 'PLAN B'

Failing to prepare is preparing to fail.

The central heating will pack up just as the next ice age begins! The garden office will disappear into a sinkhole the night before the self-assessment deadline! The Wi-Fi will go kaput just as you attempt to upload that video detailing your sinister plans for world domination!

Homeworkers need a 'Plan B' location to escape to: it could be a library, coffee shop or co-working space. Libraries are free to use and have Wi-Fi. They're also the daytime residence of a community's more eccentric characters. Our advice: never say 'yes' if offered a sandwich.

Co-working spaces charge by the day and are an excellent venue for local networking. They can, however, be populated with hyper-enthusiastic types who'll do anything to rope you into their big scheme. Learning to say: "Sorry, my workload is at capacity" is crucial.

Coffee shops with Wi-Fi, coffee and cake are the ideal place to get things done. Homeworkers should get to know the ins and outs of their coffee shop of choice (the Wi-Fi code and the location of the plug sockets). But a word of warning: watch the pennies! It's essential to master the art of nursing a small latte for hour after hour – justifying their seat in the coffee shop, without spending vast amounts of money.

BE PICKY WHO YOU TELL

The whole world may have not quite got its head around the 'working' element of the 'homeworking' role.

Homeworkers may find some of their friends, family and neighbours can't fathom that, just because they're at home all day, they're not taking a day off.

Prospective homeworkers should think carefully before announcing they're going to be home. Whether it's your very best friend, or Auntie Joan and her famed verbal diarrhoea, there's bound to be someone who just doesn't realise the inconvenience they create by persistently 'popping in'.

Unexpected visitors are a lot like vampires, they suck the lifeblood out of any homeworker's day and are almost impossible to get rid of. The key thing to remember is, like the undead, unwanted visitors need to be invited inside to become a problem: DON'T LET THEM IN! Even if it seems rude, homeworkers should hold their ground and keep interlopers on the doorstep.

The unannounced visitor isn't the only peril homeworkers face if their status becomes public knowledge. It's incredibly easy to be 'volunteered' into helping neighbours and friends with anything from 'a spot of DIY' to providing a taxi service to the airport/shops/garden centre – because if a worker is at home, it clearly means they're not busy.

GET A ROUTINE

Most of us are creatures of habit.

Friday night: chip shop supper; a present to you, from you, for surviving the week. Saturday morning: Park Run; a vain attempt to atone for the chip shop supper. Sunday evening: *The Antiques Roadshow* and a G&T; dulling the senses to the imminent arrival of Monday.

But, when the working week begins, most homeworkers don't have a structure imposed on them from above. Yes, being told what to do is frustrating, but, in order to get things done, homeworkers must create a new routine for themselves. Otherwise, the homeworker will meander aimlessly, getting nothing done – like a minor royal.

Homeworkers should set a time to be at their desk each morning and a time to finish in the evening. They should establish a lunchtime routine, including a place to eat it (i.e. not at the desk). Homeworkers should give themselves breaks during the day to drink copious amounts of very good coffee (this is of vital importance) and one 'naughty' treat per day, perhaps a nap or an episode of *Homes Under The Hammer.*

At the end of the day, when work is done, homeworkers should close the door on their workspace and not re-enter until morning. Separating the occupation from the rest of their existence is a difficult trick to pull off – and sticking to a routine can really help. Otherwise, many feel they're permanently at work – undermining the reason they chose this lifestyle in the first place.

YOU CAN NEVER HAVE TOO MANY ...

While it's not necessary to channel Tom and Barbara Good (ask your mum), homeworkers do need to be self-sufficient.

Remember the stationery cupboard in the office? Well, homeworkers no longer have access to that treasure trove. Pens, paper and printer ink, they're all down to the homeworker to supply – and you can never have too many! There's nothing worse than trying to print out the final version of a crucial document only to find there's no paper, ink or (because the kids decided to make a mosaic of SpongeBob SquarePants on the fridge door) usable sticky notes for the cover.

Anyone who works from home should make sure they're equipped with an inexhaustible supply of whatever their caffeine fix is: tea, coffee or some fancy fizzy drink. A homeworker without caffeine is like an Oasis reunion tour – a nice idea, but it's never going to work. Other essentials will deplete more quickly when homeworking begins: loo rolls for a start! Homeworkers need to make sure they don't get caught short (so to speak).

Then there's biscuits: 'It is a truth universally acknowledged that a homeworker, in possession of a tight deadline, must be in want of a custard cream'. Essentially, the homeworker becomes their own office manager. Our recommendation is to embrace the role. Why not make an 'Office Manager' badge to wear about the house? The perfect way to let everyone (the cat) know who's in charge.

THE PERFECT TIME TO (DOCTOR) DO LITTLE

Pets are great stress relievers. Having an animal in the house, combined with a non-conventional working arrangement, should make those who work from home the least-stressed people around.

Whether it's walks and feeds or grooming and games, homeworkers can do it all! Pets also provide what every homeworker secretly desires: a bit of company. Animals can mimic the role played by previous co-workers: they can be demanding (dogs), odd (parrots), oblivious to what's going on (goldfish) or simply revel in the reaction they get from acting like the homeworker isn't there (cats).

We're not saying that pets are completely without problems. Cats fall asleep on the computer keyboard just as a deadline is due. Dogs decide a big video conference is the perfect time to practise their howling, and goldfish have a habit of beaching themselves on the carpet (meaning a speedy trip to the pet shop to get an identical replacement before the kids get home).

DON'T GO ALL 'REAR WINDOW'

As the Alfred Hitchcock classic makes clear, people stuck at home all day can become fixated with the goings-on of their neighbours.

Most homeworkers spend vast amounts of time at their desk, with the same unchanging view – the day-to-day goings-on in their neighbourhood. They begin to notice the clockwork of their community's day, as folk head off to work or school, mow lawns, hang out clothes, walk dogs. The routines of others become apparent – with the homeworker seemingly the only static element in a vast machine of many moving parts. But homeworkers should avoid becoming the neighbourhood's Miss Marple. Knowing too much about their neighbours' activities won't do them any favours. Even if they suspect Mrs Jones at No. 25 is having an affair with him at No. 39, homeworkers should keep it to themselves. Similarly, if they have proof-positive that Brian across the road is letting his shire-horse-sized dog poop on his neighbour's lawn, our advice is to keep out of it. Even if a homeworker has convinced themselves that Bob at No. 9 was bumped off by his wife, in an argument over chicken Kievs, they shouldn't be too hasty in pointing the finger. Finding anything truly mysterious going on is probably just wishful thinking. We'd recommend homeworkers get away from their desk on a regular basis. A bit of fresh air usually washes away even the wildest of conspiracy theories.

PROCRASTINATION IS NOT YOUR FRIEND

Everyone suffers from the desire to procrastinate. We all put off onerous tasks by filling our time with pointless activities that make us feel (temporarily) better. Nobody in history has approached filling in a self-assessment tax return without considering a whole host of more fun activities (cleaning the toilet, defrosting the freezer, having root-canal surgery) to do instead.

Procrastination is the nemesis of those who work from home. Some homeworkers fall foul of housework, an easy time-consuming trap to fall into. They vacuum stripes into their carpets, arrange their spice racks alphabetically and scrub windows until the glass is wafer thin – anything rather than settle down to work. Others find their Achilles' heel is TV. They happily lap up the most mind-numbing programmes (*Celebrity Fish-Gutting*, *Celebrity Window-Shopping*, *Celebrities Watch Paint Dry*) rather than knuckle down to the big presentation looming over their head.

Social media is another problem for procrastinators. Checking Facebook, Instagram and Twitter can leave the homeworker with very little time to get on with whatever task it is they're actually paid to do!

We advise that procrastination is only allowed during set breaks in the homeworker's day. Watch TV, but do it at a scheduled time each morning. Clean the house, but only after you've got some tangible work done. Get on social media, but do it on the loo like everyone else!

GET DRESSED

It's all too easy for a homeworker, who won't see anyone all day, to let their standards slip. Yes, it's possible to get through a work day at home without getting washed and changed. Working in PJs sounds like fun: a glamourous idea of lounging around in silk, like a latter-day Brigitte Bardot. Don't be fooled, a ketchup-dripping bacon sandwich and a spilt coffee will inevitably transform a homeworker's pyjamas so the only person they're channelling is Bridget Jones. If a homeworker only considers making themselves presentable when there's a video call booked in, things have slipped too far.

We'd recommend a homeworker prepares for the day at home in the same way they would for a commute to a traditional office. But, of course, they're not going to be in an office so there's no need for suits and heels – unless you feel that way inclined. Freed from the tyranny of pantyhose and the pocket square, the homeworker can spend all day in their most comfortable sweatpants.

Casual is cool, but remember nothing can disguise the embarrassment when an unplanned video call reveals the homeworker is still in their PJs at three in the afternoon.

PART 3
HOME IS WHERE THE HEART IS

CELEBRATE #LYBL
(LIVING YOUR BEST LIFE)

Those who work from home are perfectly placed to live their best life.

Why?

Because it's down to the homeworker to set priorities, then shape the day to maximise upon them. So, if living their best life means modelling their existence on the picture-perfect folk of Instagram – homeworkers can achieve that!

Maybe supping Champagne over a gluten-free, locally sourced working breakfast is how a homeworker wants to live their best life? When working from home, it's so easy to accomplish! With a little effort, a partner, child or pet cat* could be trained to continually take photos of the homeworker checking emails while lounging on a fashionably distressed chaise longue, or making that important work call while delicately trimming a miniature topiary.

These images are guaranteed to show the homeworker with a relaxed glow no Instagram filter can replicate.

*A cat's lack of opposable thumbs notwithstanding.

We would, however, recommend that homeworkers limit themselves to one glass of breakfast bubbly, as getting work done like a pro (or using topiary shears) can be difficult with a fuzzy head.

If the homeworker's best life involves styling their home office so every video call depicts them at the heart of a beautifully on-trend haven of effortless accomplishment*, that's doable too.

Homeworkers have the time to achieve perfection and there's no bothersome office manager around to announce that ironic chinz is a fire risk, or that the new upcycled, William-Morris-wallpaper-covered shredder is a health and safety hazard.

*Doing this will be far from effortless, but it'll look that way on social media – which is, after all, what matters.

CELEBRATE TIME
(TO YOURSELF)

As fans of the 90s hit know, there are unlimited amounts of fun to be had when you're _Home Alone_.

An entire generation grew up thinking time alone in their house meant getting involved in the sort of hi-jinks demonstrated by Macaulay Culkin in the film.

We're not suggesting any potential homeworker should rig up mechanisms to see off intruders, but there's a glee that comes from being left alone all day that needs to be celebrated!

Homeworkers can order a
MASSIVE pizza for lunch.
Nobody will ever know.

Homeworkers can practise
their big presentation while
roller-skating in the kitchen.
Nobody will ever know.

Homeworkers can rock
to thrash metal as they
fill out their expenses.
Nobody will ever know.

Homeworkers can develop
an addiction to *The Archers*.
Nobody will ever know.

Homeworkers can spend every
Friday dressed as Spiderman.
Nobody will ever know.

NOBODY WILL EVER KNOW.

CELEBRATE WORKING TO LIVE (NOT LIVING TO WORK)

We're certain the meaning of life is not to sit in a badly designed, overcrowded office, catching colds from the air-con while listening to Ann, from finance, tell her anecdote about meeting Laurence Llewelyn-Bowen, over and over again.

So, anyone who fancies getting to grips with mindfulness and meditation should consider homeworking. People who work from home are in charge of their schedule and can make space to burn incense or master their mantra.

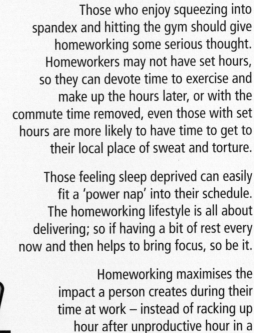

Those who enjoy squeezing into spandex and hitting the gym should give homeworking some serious thought. Homeworkers may not have set hours, so they can devote time to exercise and make up the hours later, or with the commute time removed, even those with set hours are more likely to have time to get to their local place of sweat and torture.

Those feeling sleep deprived can easily fit a 'power nap' into their schedule. The homeworking lifestyle is all about delivering; so if having a bit of rest every now and then helps to bring focus, so be it.

Homeworking maximises the impact a person creates during their time at work – instead of racking up hour after unproductive hour in a conventional office. Homeworkers work to live and this makes for a happier, more productive, employee.

If that's not something to celebrate, what is?

The homeworker's ability to change where they work, to suit their needs or mood, means they're always free to locate themselves in the perfect environment to be at their most effective.

WORK IN ... BED

John & Yoko started a revolution from their bed, so surely a homeworker can populate a spreadsheet from under the covers? All the conventions of life (getting washed, dressed, vertical, etc.) are pushed aside so it's just the homeworker and whatever they have to do. That said, homeworkers need to be careful they don't fill the bed with crumbs — turning an oasis of activity into a duvet of distraction.

WORK IN ... THE GARDEN

Wi-Fi and superfast broadband mean working outdoors is a wonderful option for homeworkers. That said, homeworkers must be vigilant against wasps, flies and other airborne nasties. Add direct sunlight (making screens impossible to decipher) and the ever-present threat of a downpour into the equation, and working in the garden isn't the recipe for relaxation it first seemed.

WORK IN ... THE BATH

Life doesn't get more decadent than a homeworker attacking the backlog in their inbox while soaking in the tub. That said, homeworkers need to be careful if their bath is set to become a workplace. Thinking about it ... the whole thing is just a bad idea, so don't do it.

Jean Paul-Sartre understood 'Hell is other people', but you don't need to be a philosopher to grasp that no longer being stuck in an office with Andy from sales (and his braying laugh) 8 hours a day, 5 days a week, is something to celebrate.

There's little to match the feeling when a homeworker realises they're no longer contractually obliged to share a confined space with a mismatched group of strangers, with nothing in common other than a palpable dislike of their boss.

Working from home means no awkward small talk at the photocopier: "I had no idea toner got used up so quickly!"

No passive-aggressive notes left in the kitchen: "The middle shelf is for the accounts team only. Will the owner of this taramasalata identify themselves?"

No obligation to give cash towards birthday presents for random co-workers: "Happy Birthday Bill – may your life be as long as an hour with you feels."

That said, not sharing an office with co-workers does mean: no more nipping out for a drink after work. No 'hilarious' card in the internal mail on the homeworker's birthday and no possibility of naughtiness in the stationery cupboard at the Christmas party.

But these are small prices to pay to avoid Sharon's coffee breath, Phil's microwaved mackerel and the ever present threat of a spontaneous team-building event!

CELEBRATE
BEING IN CHARGE
(OF EVERYTHING)

Something happens to everyone who transitions
from a conventional workplace to working
from home: they soon twig that they're in charge!

If the homeworker wants
to clock off early, they can.

If the homeworker wants to sit
in their PJs all day, they can.

If the homeworker wants to work from
2am 'til 10am every day, they can.

If the homeworker wants to park on inflatable
furniture in a polka-dot home office, they can.

If the homeworker wants to answer emails
sitting on the loo, they can.

But with great power comes great responsibility ...

If they miss a deadline,
it's the homeworker's fault.

If they don't achieve a productivity target,
it's the homeworker's fault.

If the home office ceiling falls down,
it's the homeworker's problem.

If their phone falls down the toilet,
it's the homeworker's problem.

**Yes, there are downfalls to the homeworking life,
but let's be honest – if it's possible, it's the way to go.**

ABOUT US

Spencer Wilson is a homeworker of sorts.
Working from his studio in Hertfordshire, Spencer illustrates and designs whilst watching a line of grumpy commuters trundle by. Spencer loves every aspect of studio life, apart from the cold winter months when he has to consume his body weight in biscuits each day to stay warm ... a hardship he takes squarely on the chin. A keen cyclist, Spencer uses the extra time working from 'home' brings as an opportunity to talk about getting out on his bike. Whilst some of the experiences depicted in this book are based on his life, Spencer would like to point out he doesn't drink piña coladas every Friday afternoon*.

*He prefers a craft lager.

 @spencerwilson8

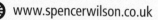 www.spencerwilson.co.uk

Chris McGuire is a homeworker.
After an award-winning career in TV, Chris now works at home as a writer and stay-at-home dad. Chris loves most aspects of homeworking: the freedom, the easy access to the fridge and the close proximity of his bed – to name a few. If he could change anything about working from home it would be the assumption Chris watches *This Morning* all day – he doesn't, it's not on in the afternoons.

Although many of the experiences outlined in this book are based on events in Chris' life, he would like to point out that he doesn't spend Fridays in his home office, dressed as Spiderman*.

*He does this on a Tuesday.

@McGuireski

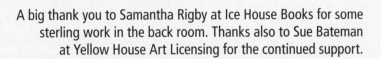

A big thank you to Samantha Rigby at Ice House Books for some sterling work in the back room. Thanks also to Sue Bateman at Yellow House Art Licensing for the continued support.